The
Big Brother's
Guide
to
Job Interviews

The Big Brother's Guide to Job Interviews

DR. DAVID A. BISHOP

NVR Publishers

Contact: New York Research Publishers

http://www.nyrpublishers.com

Copyright © 2018 David A. Bishop

All rights reserved.

978-0-9998160-2-8

978-0-9998160-3-5

DEDICATIONS

To all of my mentees, I hope this helps you become a better interviewer, and enriches your personal and professional life.

TABLE OF CONTENTS

CHAPTER ONE

INTRODUCTION: WHY I WROTE THIS BOOK

I n my over 25 years of managing and mentoring people in the technology industry, handling job interviews is one of the highest topics of concern for most people I talk to. After attending and conducting countless interviews on both sides of the hiring table, I developed a list of Interview Do's and Don'ts that go far past the typical "dress well and be prepared" advice peddled by so many writers on the topic. Indeed, in my experience I discovered that most successful interviewers did much more than what I have read in most books on job interviewing. They were skilled at attending to the delicate nuances of what was happening during the interview, and quickly adapted.

I found that not only are there more aesthetic things you can do to ensure your interview success, but there are also key characteristics to indicate whether a job interview is "good" or not or even worth your time attending. By following the advice in this book, you will have a better chance at getting the job you want, reducing time spent on "bad" opportunities so you can focus on the "good" ones, and handling "crisis" situations during the interview process that throw many candidates off track, turning what would have been a good interview into a bad experience.

One thing this book is not, is a technical interview guide, for example, helping programmers answer the right technical questions during a job interview. I've found that often, these "technical questions" are not the "make or break" determinant in getting the job, rather, the real determinants are more about personality and social fit which is what we will discuss here. This is also an area where most interviewees fall short, especially technical professionals.

As alluded to earlier, another thing this book is not, is "just another guide for interviews". There are several books available that discuss job interviewing. However, with the Big Brother series, we focus on providing "uncommon knowledge" about these topics that aren't as widely disseminated. Your "big brother" is going to arm you with advice that you don't typically find in a mass-produced book. Advice based on real-life experience at all levels of employment, from individual contributor roles to executive. My hope is that this will give you a competitive edge over the other candidates. In today's hyper-competitive job market, this can make a huge difference in your professional career. Enjoy!

CHAPTER TWO

INTERVIEWING IN TODAY'S GLOBALIZED ECONOMY

When I first started in this business as a fresh graduate over twenty-five years ago, the economy was booming, and opportunities in the tech sector seemed like they would never end. I remember posting my résumé to a job site on the internet, and getting barraged with calls for days, and this was back when I had nowhere near the experience I have today. After 2001, all of that changed, and even though the job market has ebbed and flowed through the years, it has since slowly become more competitive and strained. Companies are focused on hiring the cheapest person that can do the job, and hiring managers are often more concerned about being ousted by a new hire than bringing in top talent. Add in the practice of outsourcing many jobs overseas, and you have a tight, highly competitive job market. The downside to this is that the job you wanted may not offer the benefits and long-term security that you hoped it would, but the upside is that this market forces you to be the best you can be, and can bring out talents, skills, and abilities in you that otherwise you could be too "fat, dumb, and happy" to discover.

In this market, you are selling yourself. You are the product. And just like selling any other product out there, you must do a market analysis on yourself and define your position. In this chapter we will do just that, by taking you through the steps of self-discovery as it pertains to your competitive position and career goals.

Knowing Yourself

The first step to good interviewing is knowing yourself, so you can establish realistic goals, and figure out what kind of opportunities you should pursue.

What do you want to do?

Ok, here's where the "rubber meets the road" so to speak. What is it that you really want to do? You need to make sure that you have a genuine interest in the position that you decide to pursue. If that interest isn't there, you either won't have the determination to stick with the plan or be happy with what you've done. This genuine interest will not only be evident to some degree in your résumé, but, more importantly, will show through during interviews.

Your Experience

Let's start with what you have done. If you have any experience at all, it is best to find some way to build on it. Perhaps you've been a manager before? Even though it had nothing to do with technology, the organizational and people skills you obtained could make you an excellent project manager or team lead. Use them! Maybe you are good with PC's, windows, home networking, or some combination. You could make use of those skills as a help desk analyst, PC tech, or even windows administrator.

Skill Targeting

Job descriptions always include a minimum "skill set". Often, the reason the position is open in the first place is because they lack the proper talent or "skill set" in their current organization. By carefully reading the job description, and listening during the interview process, you can often narrow this down to a special "skill" or skill combination that the employer is looking for. Read the job description, is there an application or skill that is mentioned more than once? Does the description list a "must have" or an "absolute requirement"? What about "pluses"? Tailor your résumé so that you have all the required skills...be sure the special skill is mentioned throughout. When you interview, be prepared to answer questions on those skills, and be sure to emphasize any "pluses" that the employer is looking for. Pay attention to what they ask you...if they ask you about a certain skill more than once, try to hinge on that and expand on it. Make the employer feel secure that you have what they want. Use these skills to justify your salary request. Mention these skills each time your salary is questioned!

Hard skills vs. Soft skills

Next, we need to take a look at your skills. First, we need to break them down in terms of hard skills and soft skills. Both are needed to be fully successful. You need to do a careful examination of yourself to figure out which you are best at, and what you need to work on. This is largely determined by your level of professional development. For example, if you are applying for a job in Information Technology but are relatively new to this industry, then you definitely need to concentrate on hard skills, which could be windows administration, networking, java programming, etc. For those of you experienced in IT and looking to advance, it is probably your lack of soft skills that is holding you back. Good communication skills, ability to work with people, and leadership skills, are all important for advancement. The same could be said for almost any profession, each requires certain levels of hard and soft skills. Increasingly, job descriptions today are putting emphasis on soft skills. Is that because "tech heads" are often considered lacking in this area? Yes, to an extent. But it is also a by-product of today's litigious and hyper-sensitive society. Due to the mix of cultures, backgrounds, value systems, and languages, getting along with people productively is a bigger challenge than ever in the workplace.

Education and Experience

You don't always have to have a lot of education. Especially in today's market, experience is often accepted in lieu of education. However, it is becoming harder than ever to stand out from the crowd, so every little bit helps. It's always good to have just a little bit more than what's required. If a Computer Science degree is needed for the job, those who have Electrical or Computer Engineering degrees will not only be interviewed more favorably, but also get higher offers. Remember, pay is often based on education and experience. If 5 years of experience is required, try to show that you have 8-10 years. In terms of experience, there are several barriers...the "entry-level barrier" the "five-year barrier" and the "ten-year barrier". Most jobs fall into one of these three experience categories. Once you break each barrier, your potential salary will grow. Unfortunately, this growth tends to slowdown and decline as we get past forty years of age as experience begins to be looked upon negatively by employers after this point, but that's another issue altogether.

Industry Research: Going straight to the company you desire

Based on your location requirements, career goals, and skillset, you should identify a list of companies that have positions you are interested in. These will be your target companies. Job searches usually work best if you can target specific companies or positions.

Set on one particular company? That's ok, but it severely limits your potential prospects. Perhaps there are a few large companies that you are particularly interested in. The first step is to go ahead and send your résumé and application to them via their website. No, you probably won't get a response right away, but you should do it. The next thing you need to do is try to get face time with a decision-maker. Do the following:

- Research the company. Find out names of managers or at least the name of the corporate recruiter.
- Keep your eyes and ears open for job fairs that the company may be holding. This will be a great chance to get hold of someone face to face.

- Get to know someone with the company if you don't already. Ask them to refer you. Many companies pay referral fees to employees, so they may be more than happy to take your résumé.
- Make as many phone calls, send as many résumés and cover letters as it takes to get yourself in front of a person who can make a difference for you. By and large, the jobs fair or referral will be the best method. But anything can happen.

In the following chapters, I will reveal some real-life experiences that I hope will prove invaluable to you. This is followed by a quick start preparation guide that summarizes all the critical items you need to know to be successful in your interviewing venture. The book is then summarized with a series of Do's and Don'ts based on tried and true experiences, and some last-minute advice on some "avant-garde" techniques that could get you out of a jam!

CHAPTER THREE

INTERVIEWS FROM HELL

In my 20 years of experience in IT I've interviewed a lot...and I've learned a great deal about human nature, how to size up an organization quickly, and determine whether I'm going to get (or even want) the job in question. If you're like me, you love reading about and learning from other people's experiences. This section discusses some of my most interesting job interviews and what I gained from them.

The Abusive Interviewer

Some of the worst interviews I had took place early in my career, as a fresh graduate. For many people at that stage, your first source of interviews is the career services department at your alma mater. As such, many schools place rules on how these interviews are conducted. Candidates must arrive on time, dress a certain way, and not do anything that would tick off the interviewer. A complaint could ruin your chances of getting more interviews. So, I signed up with my school's career services office to get interviews...companies would come onsite to the school and students could express interest and then the company would select candidates. This is one interview

I will never forget. I met with an HR lady from a large telecom company, and she invited me onsite for an all-day interview shindig. I was excited...this was one of the first real job interviews I ever had. She had lamented that I was the only person from my school who was interested in their company...which surprised me a bit.

When I arrived, there were several candidates, mostly new graduates like me, being interviewed. We sat there and watched presentations about the company and the benefits. Then we were taken to lunch by a group of employees. All I remember is that one of the ladies that took us had a ton of piercings, mostly in her nose. I thought that her piercings looked quite out of place on her otherwise conservative business attire. When we came back, we were each sent off to interview separately with three interviewers. The first was an older guy who was very impressed with me. The second was with a fellow who spent the entire time simply making small talk...as if he was trying to make me comfortable. The third was a short guy who was nice at first but became a monster once I mentioned the school I was from. At this point I had been a graduate for probably less than a week. I had little to talk about except my school experience, which was essentially no experience. I wasn't trying to be arrogant about my school, I just had nothing much to talk about except my college classes and experience. But he seemed to take offense to this and said, "well I went to Clemson!!!" and proceeded to berate me and my school. I can't remember the details, only that he was very insulting and started asking me questions about their own operations that I couldn't possibly know. He took me on a brief tour and then back to the room where the HR lady and others were sitting. He smiled at me devilishly. I was upset and angry at the way he had treated me. We were then given a test to take, a programming test, and I didn't do well on it because I was so upset. I went through the motions for the rest of the day and never said anything. The school had drilled into us that if they ever got any complaints about us, they wouldn't send us on any more interviews.

I should have said something though...I could have easily gotten him into trouble. He had no business interviewing young students.

INTERVIEW LESSON #1: DON'T PUT UP WITH ABUSE UNDER ANY CIRCUMSTANCES!! Leave! Walk out and let HR or the person's manager know about it! Period! And when someone starts that crap, you're not going to get the job anyway so get up and leave. You are wasting your time. It's not going to get better.

The Bad Manager

Years ago, I interviewed for a large credit reporting firm. I got the interview through a recruiter. The manager was a fat red-headed guy who was neurotic, shaky, and unsure of himself. He was obsessed with testing me. He stated that he had to interview me thoroughly because they had just fired a guy that couldn't do the job - RED FLAG!! He said that every time he looked over this guy's shoulder, he noticed he was doing something wrong.

So already, I knew this was a job I didn't want. The manager just fired a guy for incompetence - if the guy wasn't incompetent then the manager was probably a worrywart and a pain to work for. If he was incompetent, then it's still a bad reflection on the manager for hiring him in the first place. Plus, would you want your boss looking over your shoulder every minute of the day? I could just picture this guy standing behind me every minute...who wouldn't be nervous? Who wouldn't make a mistake under those conditions?

So, he gave me a thorough technical interview...he got up and left twice - each time he came back in and said, "I just want to ask you a few more questions..." I thought "My God!!" He then gave me a test to take, and said someone would be coming in a few minutes to give me yet another technical interview.

As soon as the guy walked out the room I got up and left. I told the HR lady that I was no longer interested and that I didn't want to go forward, and she became irate with me and called the recruiter agency and complained. I should have told her the details and how I felt...but I didn't want to hurt anyone, I did not want to tell her that I thought the manager was incompetent...I just told her I wasn't interested. I didn't want to waste any more of my time.

INTERVIEW LESSON #2: Be careful of situations where you are replacing someone who just got terminated. Where there's smoke, there's fire...and often, the company and management are just as guilty as the guy who got canned. Be on guard when asked to take a test. That's a sure sign that there have been "problems" and you don't want to work somewhere that has had "problems". Any manager worth his salt should be able to size someone up and determine whether they can do the job or not.

The Test

Several years ago, I interviewed with a small company that asked me to take a test. The company started with an "O", and I can't remember the name now. But they went on and on over the phone about how hard this test was, and how important it was. The company seemed to have a great deal of pride regarding this test and its ability to weed out people. I got the interview through a head hunter who spent a lot of time talking to me about this stupid test and how many people had flunked it or not done very well.

I spent about three hours or longer taking this damn test before I spoke to hardly anyone...then I turned it in and waited. The HR lady came out and told me that I had made the highest score ever on the exam. She went on and on about how well I did. I was so proud!! Wow I thought...this is a slam dunk job offer!! I was then taken to an older gentleman to interview me. He appeared nervous and asked me about pay....my request at the time wasn't very high. But he told me that they couldn't come close to my salary requirements. He pointed to two guys across the hall and said, "he's been here x number of years and only makes such and such". He wouldn't even make me an offer. Not a single question was asked.

Another total waste of time. The recruiter had verified with me beforehand the salary requirements...it shouldn't have been a problem.

INTERVIEW LESSON #3: NEVER EVER take a damn test. The best jobs I've had never required a test. A test is a red flag. In this case, I don't know if I was that far above the salary requirements or if this guy just didn't want to hire me for some crazy reason. Either way, it was a serious waste of my time. There's an old saying that goes something along the lines of avoiding battles where you have no potential to gain anything. Taking a test gains you nothing. If you don't do well enough, you are eliminated on the spot after spending a LOT of time. If you do well, at best, you'll be advanced to the next hiring phase, but it won't make a big difference for you. It is a sign that the company has problems, that it has been sued or accused of unfair hiring practices, or there is low confidence among the decision-makers about their ability to size up people. There are a few small exceptions to this, as with certain programming jobs, but that is rare.

The Caribbean Banking Interview

This was another one I got through my school...this was over twenty years ago of course. I can't remember the name, but it was a small company situated in a tiny South Georgia town called "Hahira", not far from the Florida border. I had a phone interview with a gentleman from down there, and had cancelled an interview with them once already. I had wised up about wasting my time with these go-nowhere interviews, and I was still kind of a lazy college student. Even after I blew them off, they kept calling me back. They offered to put me up in a hotel and everything. Eventually I decided to take them up on the interview and make the long drive down there. Unfortunately, I had gotten up late and didn't arrive on time. This was a long time ago when I was much younger.

The office was downtown in what looked like an old bank building. When I arrived, I was situated in a big room and waited. Apparently, the guy I talked to on the phone had already given up on me and left. A young lady came out to interview me. It went well, and she appeared to like me for a co-worker. After some conversation she showed me around a bit...the building looked like it was falling apart in some places. Plaster hanging down...workers were situated in these little cubby-holes. It was truly a weird operation.... almost hidden. The company basically developed banking software for banks in the

Caribbean islands. Curacao was one of their biggest customers. Visits to the islands were common. They went on about how cool it was to "lay out on the beach" while you worked. She then took me to interview with the manager, who was rude to me. Can't remember much detail, only that he seemed bent from the get-go not to hire me. It seemed that my lateness had spoiled everything, which wasn't a surprise and somewhat justified. I don't suppose I'd have hired me either. The girl who I had been talking to seemed as if she was trying to convince the manager to hire me...she then looked at me sadly as the manager began to give me a hard time, laughing and sneering at my answers.

I was then asked to sit and wait for a while to see if anyone else would be interviewing me.... she later came out and released me. I left a form for the receptionist about being reimbursed for my mileage and I got a check quickly. I was going to make sure I got compensated for my time this go around.

INTERVIEW LESSON #4: I really didn't want this job...these little Podunk operations scared me at the time. I've since found out that these little Caribbean islands had questionable banking practices. I'm not sure if there was a link...but who knows. I interviewed for this job because I was unemployed and a little desperate at the time...I needed money badly. Check out the company before you go, and if you really aren't interested in the job, don't go. It will show. You don't want your time wasted, so don't waste theirs. In my defense, I would say that at the time our school encouraged us to go on as many interviews as possible to gain practice, which was why I followed through.

The Home Business Interview

This was a good one.

In this example, the company was called "assistant coach software" or something like that. I don't even think it exists anymore. The software had some way of tracking a player's performance. Mostly with basketball as I recall. I interviewed with a young man at the school and the interview went very well. He seemed very professional and later, called me back to schedule a follow-up interview with the "others".

I was given a residential address and told to dress "casual". The interview was at someone's home. I was greeted at the door by the owner of the company and his wife. There were only three people in this company...the guy I interviewed with at school, the CEO, and some guy that worked offsite who "helped them out" whom I would probably never see. They expressed some chagrin at the way I was dressed. I was wearing jeans, and I guess they thought I should have dressed "business casual", meaning khakis and a polo. Back then I was just a college kid and thought that casual was casual...heck, I was going to someone's house for God's sake!

They took me down to the basement where they worked...a few computers were setup there. They showed me the software and how it worked, and we talked shop for a while. They basically needed someone to do visual basic coding. Something I was keen on at the time. This was when the web was in its infancy. Client/server apps were still all the rage.

Then, they took me for a ride in their car...I can't remember the justification they gave for "going for a ride" but I do remember they made a point of stopping by the bank and depositing a big check. They had an account with ESPN at the time. Or so they said. I guess this was supposed to impress me and give me a sense of security. They went on about how cool it was to have a job that combined sports and computers and how much fun they had. Anyway, the whole thing creeped me out a bit and I suppose they could tell. The interview overall seemed to go well but I didn't get the job. No technical questions were asked of course...they just wanted to get to know me. As I recall, I believe the rejection letter said something about not filling the job. I think they just decided they didn't need anyone.

INTERVIEW LESSON #5: Don't waste your time with a one-horse company unless you really believe it's a good opportunity, know the people involved, or are just downright desperate. Don't go to someone's house either, unless you know them. This is especially true if you are a young person. Do as much research up-front as you can. When this happened to me, the web was in its infancy and there were few options to vet a company. This kind of thing probably wouldn't happen much today, since the internet offers a plethora of ways to verify whether a company is legit. Just be on your guard.

The Soda Company Interview

About ten years ago I interviewed for an IT Director position with a large soda manufacturer. I interviewed with five people, including the CIO. They had several candidates appearing that day, and we spent quite some time lazing about in the lounge area until we were called.

Much of the interview is blurry now.... but I do remember the most important points. I spoke with the HR person. This went smooth enough...but I remember he made a statement that one person may be a difficult interviewer because she was somewhat eccentric. So, I knew right away where the challenge was. This lady was also the key decision-maker. As I later found out, this new position was designed to "help out" this director who was apparently swamped with work. They needed to split her position. I knew right away this wasn't going to happen.

I interviewed with another director, who remarked about my long hair and youthful appearance, but did so in a positive way, stating that he wished they had more like me working there. Next, was a project manager - who was obviously a friend of the IT director I'd be working closely with. They interviewed me together, and their line of questioning was only concerned with one thing - how easy or difficult I would be to work with. I answered each question decisively, as they picked and pored to find something wrong with me. Most of the questions centered on my current job and why I wanted to leave there. The truth was I was interviewing for a higher position and more pay, but I couldn't tell them that. If I had, the interview would have been over right then and there. No one likes to see someone reach above their station, although we do it all the time. The final gavel came down when the IT director asked me if I knew Galen, (not his real name of course) a friend of mine who worked at one of my previous companies on my résumé. I knew him very well and said so. Unfortunately, unbeknownst to me, my friend didn't stay there very long and quit after only a year. He went back to work for the airline that he came from. Now, I love my friend, but I knew that he was the kind of guy that couldn't handle stress and change very much. His constitution was nothing like mine. Nevertheless, this lady made the snap decision that she would have the same experience with me as she did with him, and as a result I was not hirable. During the interview she fluttered around, acted all stressed, and stared at me constantly. She seemed afraid of me. I was smart, young, and capable. Her worst nightmare.

I interviewed with the CIO which went nicely enough...the only thing I remember is that I mentioned something about "fixing problems" and he replied defensively, "we have no problems here!". Every IT organization has problems. They are riddled with them. This guy was not living in the real world. But like many people in this position, they are not looking to make a difference, they only want to "ride the wave" and gather their bonuses until the next opportunity comes along. Within a year or two, the CIO was gone.

Anyways, I didn't get the job, in fact, no one did. Several rounds of additional interviews took place with other candidates until they eventually killed the position. The bottom line was that the IT Director didn't want anyone hired.... she didn't really need any help at all...she just wanted to make her management think she did. She was worried about keeping her job and didn't want any competition. This is a tactic used by many people in this business, and it often backfires. In a vain attempt to make herself appear indispensable, she made herself look too busy to take on additional work. This forced the company to hire help, because the work has got to get done, regardless of individual sensibilities. However, this made her even more frightened, because a new person could be a threat to her security. She would no longer be indispensable. As a result, she deep-sixed the interview process. It took a while, but HR and her management eventually realized that they didn't need to fill the job at all. However, myself and many others wasted a LOT of personal time to prepare and attend multiple all-day interviews. WE paid the expense for one person's hubris.

INTERVIEW LESSON #6: Find out before the interview if this is a newly-created position. Ask (before the interview if you can) why this job is being created and what the long-term plans are for it? Try to determine the seriousness of the company to fill the job. By asking a few questions, you can usually quickly tell if the interview is a waste of time or not. Be aware if you are ever told that one of the interviewers is "special", or "eccentric" in some way. This is often code for "problematic" and if you get the job at all, you could be in for a rough time. My friend was a smart guy, but this director's haphazard and disorganized management method drove him crazy. It was her way of covering up for her inadequacies.

Small companies

Small companies can provide unique interview experiences and situations. Small companies are limited in budget and resources, and will try to put the squeeze on any role that is considered an expense or "cost center". Information Technology is a necessary component for almost every business today, but for small companies that see it as an expense or inconvenience rather than an asset, interviewing for such roles can be a challenge. You need to be aware, if you take a job with such an organization, what you are in for. I'm going to walk you through two examples to illustrate my point.

Many years ago, I interviewed for a CIO position with a small trucking company. The fellow who had the job currently was about to retire, and they needed to replace him. I spent some time interviewing with the old gent and he was very nice. We hit it off well. As we toured the facility, I noted the old equipment and haphazard wiring around the place. The incumbent lamented the fact that he did not have the time or resources to do a better job of things. This was the first red flag that I noticed. This guy might have been old, but he was smart and good at his job. He was being run ragged fixing broken printers and computer monitors that were on the blink and as a result did not have time to put into building the e-commerce website the company wanted, and was barely able to keep the financial and scheduling systems online. The only help he had was another older gentleman, who I was told was also a possible candidate for the job in question. The interview with him went quite well though, as did the interview with the COO. The Operations officer in particular was interested in my background and my ability to get the financial and operations systems upgraded and running more efficiently. Apparently, they had a large failure of these applications recently which took their business offline and caused some financial loss. I figured out that this event was probably the impetus for the current CIO's "retirement".

I then interviewed with the CEO himself. This was where it went downhill. This guy had a serious inferiority complex, despite having a Harvard MBA and getting his undergrad from the same school as me. After reviewing my résumé, he began asking me all sorts of strange questions. He stated that he knew their work environment was not quite as nice as where I was currently working, and wondered if I would be ok with that. I told him that the cubicles or "digs" as many people called them did not make much difference to me. It was all about the job. He kept asking me questions about why I wanted to work there and what I planned to do once I started. He emphasized the lack of budget they had for Information Technology. I told him that many consulting firms would charge outrageous rates to do what I could accomplish for a fraction of the cost. I outlined a high-level plan to him on hiring a couple of inexpensive PC techs to provide technical support, and an upgrade plan for their antiquated systems and website. I was trying to show my enthusiasm for the job, but for some reason, the more excited I appeared, the more scared this guy got. During one of these questions, he asked again why I wanted to work there and I told him I wanted to make a difference. He responded with "well, we do not need someone who wants to be famous" or something to that effect, and then sent me to the human resources person. As he guided me to her office, he whispered something to her and then left. As I sat down she immediately took an attitude with me, and stated "you look too young for this job, how old are you?". I was about thirty-five at the time. She then stated that "we needed someone older for the job". I couldn't believe what I was hearing. She asked me if I was married, and if I had any children.

All of this was a blatant violation of EEOA statutes. This interview was short, and I was then passed along to the old CIO. He took me outside and grilled me about what the CEO had asked me. He asked if the CEO was ticked off and I said that I could not really tell, because I did not know him well enough. The CIO wanted me to have the job, he understood why I wanted to move, but apparently the CEO thought that I was a threat to him in some way, and did not want a young, smart, motivated person working for him. Not in Information Technology at least.

In this example, I was probably the best candidate for the job, based on what the CIO told me. However, the CEO did not want that. He only wanted a hamster that would jump in the wheel and jog. He did not want better, he wanted status quo. What the human resources person did was a blatant legal violation. I should have called them on that, but I did not. I had gotten the interview via a support group through my school, and did not want to burn any bridges. However, looking back on it I think I should have. I was firmly in the right to do so.

INTERVIEW LESSON #7: Don't look too eager or enthusiastic with small companies or organizations. This sounds counterintuitive, but it's the truth today. The only time they want an enthusiastic person is when you are entry-level, because at that point you can't be a threat to anyone and they know they can work you to death for nothing. Don't put up with obvious interview abuse either. If you experience it, you will almost certainly not get the job anyway, so you have nothing to lose by reporting it.

Another similar experience was an interview with a small pharmaceutical manufacturer. This company manufactured drugs according to its client's specifications. The workforce consisted of scientists, chemists, factory personnel, a number of business and sales people, and one lonely guy in IT. I had gotten the interview through a recruiter firm, and the first thing they told me was that the company was trying to fire the current IT manager, but they wanted to keep it a secret from him. This was the first red flag.

I was met onsite by a manager from the recruiting agency who gave me a hard time, looking over my suit and presentation as if I was a kid out of school or something. The human resources lady was my guide, and most of my day was spent with her. They proceeded to explain that for years, the IT in the company was managed by one man, who had retired years ago, and the current manager was someone they had recently hired from the outside. Apparently, he recently had some kind of failure with a document management system that cost the company a lot of money, and that was enough for them to get rid of him. The entire IT infrastructure was being held together by popsicle sticks and chewing gum by Tom, a young man who was the son of the previous long-time manager before the new guy came on board. The HR lady whisked me from room to room, emphasizing the fact that she did not want the IT manager to see me. I talked to just about every leader in the company, including all the C-level executives. In this position, I would be reporting to the CFO, who seemed ready to hire me on the spot. Two other executives, in sales and product management, were also excited to see me there. One gentleman asked me about having "intellectual curiosity" with respect to IT, and of course, I had quite a lot of that. What did not make sense was that he wasn't talking about e-commerce or networking communications, he was referring to PC support.

Apparently, a big part of the job consisted of running around from PC to PC fixing one little problem after another. Nobody wants to do that. Why would you pay someone a six-figure salary to reboot PCs and reload printers all day? This became a larger and larger issue as the discussions went on. The HR lady said that she had to "take calls about benefits" from employees all the time which was something she didn't like to do. I told her that PC support is a time-consuming but simple job. A couple of young, talented techs could handle most of these problems without breaking the bank. The reason this was such a big issue was that everyone throughout the company had different PC configurations, software, operating systems, patch levels, etc. This all needed to be consistent to reduce costs and increase efficiency. It was a hodgepodge thrown together and it was a big mess. I outlined a plan with the COO that would correct this issue, but he was paranoid about cost. He stated how they had been ripped off by consultants before, and I then told him that I was not a consultant, that as an employee I could do this for a fraction of what a 3rd-party would charge. He then started in on the "visibility" tip. He wanted to make sure I would do what he (the COO) wanted and give that high priority over what the other execs asked for. Here's where the problem was. The current IT manager was supporting the efforts of some of the other execs against the COO, who was the key decision-maker. It was all a political power play, and the IT manager role was seen as someone who could upset the balance of power within the company. The CEO and founder was nothing more than a figurehead, with the COO running the show. It was interesting that as important as the IT manager was, there was no CIO role. That would be considered another threat. They wanted to keep the position, and therefore, the person in it, very weak, yet they needed someone to solve all their problems. They wanted to eat their cake and to have it as well.

The interview lasted all day long. I went to lunch with the HR lady and then returned for more interviews. By the end of the day I was exhausted. They rattled on and on about their IT problems, and all I could think of was how simple they were to fix, with the proper staff, software, and management in place. After being dismissed, I talked to my rep at the head hunter firm the next day. I did not get the job. She became upset and started screaming at her boss about how many people they had sent out to this client, how long they kept me there, and how many problems this company had. She did not want to do business with them again, and neither did I.

INTERVIEW LESSON #8: Whenever you are interviewing for a job that is not part of the company's main business, but is a necessary evil, like Information Technology, the advancement and growth opportunities can be severely limited. Where there's smoke, there's fire. Stay away from political dramas. Not getting this job was a blessing for me. It would have been a veritable Peyton place for sure.

CHAPTER FOUR

INTERVIEWS FROM HEAVEN

Not all interviews are bad, in fact most are pretty good. They would have to be, otherwise none of us would be hired! In this section, I'll be highlighting interviews that may not have necessarily resulted in an offer, but were conducted in a mostly positive fashion. They were interviews that I learned something positive from despite the situations they put me in. I hope you will learn from them as well.

Getting Past Blockers

Once, when I applied to work for a major airline, I sent my résumé numerous times to the human resources contact there with no response. I wanted the job, because all the requirements fit me like a "T". When the HR person finally called, she was short and obtuse. There was something in my background that she did not like, but would not say what it was. She gave me the "we'll call you when we're ready" line. Not long after that, I went to a job fair, and it just so happened this airline was one of the attending companies. I had made note of the companies present at this fair, and made the proper preparations. When I walked up to the airline's booth, I went into my elevator speech, showed them my résumé, and mentioned the job I was interested in. Not only were human resources and recruiters there, but also the hiring manager for the job I was targeting! The person at the booth quickly grabbed the hiring manager and gave her my résumé. As she looked at it, I could tell she was interested. I politely mentioned that I had contacted HR before and spoke to someone. They then brought out the human resources manager, who had overseen the position. It was the same person who I had tried to contact before. She glanced at my résumé, mumbled something about seeing it before, and gave me a wary gleam. However, the hiring manager was hooked, and a job interview and offer quickly followed.

I ended up not taking the offer, because the human resources manager would not give me the "senior level" position and compensation I wanted. I ended up going with someone else, but six months later, a new HR rep at the airline called me unexpectedly with another offer, this time giving me what I wanted. The previous person who had blocked me for so long had quit. This turned out to be one of the best jobs I had.

INTERVIEW LESSON #9: Don't let blockers stop you. I kept trying, because I just had a feeling that the job was right for me. Now, I got lucky with the job fair situation which allowed me to bypass the blocker. But things change over time, so someone who is trying to stop you today could (and most likely will) be gone tomorrow.

This begs the question, why does this "blocking" activity occur? It usually has to do with either jealousy, money, or both. People who have positions of power over others often impose their own misguided value system at the expense of the company. You would think that they would simply do their job and find the best candidate for the position, but all too often, many people get religious about it. They may dislike the school you went to, maybe you are a threat to a friend of theirs in the same group for which you are applying, you are asking for more money than what the others are making, or for some crazy reason they simply do not want to see someone like you succeed. When confronted with these situations, you need to find a way to bypass this person, avoid putting them on alert, and don't give them a reason to dislike you.

Dealing with Head Hunters

Over the years, I've gotten several jobs via headhunters (professional recruiters), both good and bad ones. Whether or not this is the case often depends on the head hunter and their attitude towards job candidates and the field in general. There are two types. The ones who like what they do and respect the professional candidates they work with, and the ones who are filled with jealousy and loathing for the "tech heads" they have to deal with every day. Unfortunately, I've found the latter to be much more common. The best interviews I've had with head hunters have been those where the recruiter and I had a good relationship. All too often, when we contact a head hunter or recruiter, we see them as a barrier and whiz by their questions to convince them we are viable enough to pass along to their clients. Spend more time with them. I got a good job in the utility industry because I took the time to get to know the recruiter. He also took an interest in me. He had a personal relationship with the hiring manger and was actually trying to get the best candidate. This is rare, but you can find these people if you look hard enough. In virtually every head hunter recruiting situation I had, most turned sour except for two, and these two opportunities were obtained through good people that respected me and took the time to get to know me. Do this when you interface with them and see if they reciprocate. If you find yourself getting into a long conversation with a recruiter, it's almost like a good date, you have a good feeling about it and the relationship will pay dividends in the future.

Once it came interview time, I was practically a shew in. I interviewed with four people, but they had few questions. It was clear the decision had already been made, thanks in no small part to the recruiter.

INTERVIEW LESSON #10: Develop close relationships with a few good recruiters. Most are hacks, but there are a few good ones out there, and they have access to a lot of jobs. Look for those that are detail-oriented and respectful of you. If they treat you that good, then they probably treat their paying clients even better, and those are the best recruiters.

Taking a step down, to get a leg up

As most people will tell you, government jobs don't pay as well as private companies. There is evidence that some of this is changing, but I believe that in most instances this still holds true. Despite the low pay, government entities usually have better retirement benefits, and as a result have an older average workforce. On the plus side, a government position can provide greater job security and advancement opportunity for those willing to take the chance. Many years ago, I took that chance. I interviewed for and accepted an IT management job overseeing 21 people for a government agency. I interviewed with the CIO, COO, and another manager. I thought the interview was difficult and that it had not gone well, but I was surprised a few days later when an offer was made. I had not managed that many people before. I was going to be responsible for pretty much all IT in the agency except the data centers and mainframes. The work load was daunting, and the pay was pitiful, but I was ready for a challenge, so I accepted it. I learned enough in that job to fill an entire book. The one thing I want you to take away from this is that in some cases, if you want to get a leg up on your career, you may have to take a step down pay-wise for a short time in order to get there.

INTERVIEW LESSON #11: The best opportunities don't always have an immediate payoff.

The Company X Interviews

I once interviewed with a very large software company whom I will refer to here as "company x". I had two entirely separate interview sessions with company x for two very different jobs. This was about ten years ago. Company x has a somewhat unique approach to interviewing and hiring candidates. I had made initial contact with the company via a local job fair sponsored by my university. The recruiter I worked with loved my background and thought I would be a great fit for an opening they had. After a couple of weeks, I was given instructions to apply for the job online. One thing I noticed was the job description was very short and vague. I had little concern about it though because I had discussed the job and my background extensively with the recruiter who recommended me. This was followed by a phone interview with two managers, which went very well. I was not asked many technical questions. As with most jobs these days, they were focused on personality and "fit". A person is generally considered a good "fit" if their personality, background, and perceived intellectual capacity closely match the others on the team. I do remember that the interviewers were upbeat and excited to have me come onsite for an interview. Travel was arranged and paid for by the company and I was whisked out to Redmond.

The schedule was an all-day affair. I arrived the night before and my first appointment was scheduled for 8am in the morning. The time difference between east and west coast was challenging for me. I had a hard time getting enough sleep. For dinner, I found a local BBQ restaurant. It was the only one in town. I called and asked them if they served Memphis, Kansas City, Texas, or Carolina style BBQ. The waitress responded "uh, it's just BBQ". I decided to play it safe and order pizza. The first interview was with the two managers, which went very well. They seemed very happy to have me there. I then interviewed with two project managers, one of which seemed more junior level and the other more senior. In talking with them about the job, I began to notice that many roles and responsibilities at company x were somewhat unique and/or very different from most other companies I had worked at (and I have worked for many). For example, the senior project manager knew nothing about the Project Management Institute (PMI) or PMP certification, which is almost an industry standard. Their job did not seem to consist of managing projects at all, at least not in the traditional sense; they were more or less paper pushers or what some would call, project coordinators.

I then moved on to have lunch with the technical lead, a tall lanky fellow with a sour attitude. I overheard him briefly arguing with the two managers whom I had talked to earlier as they came down the hall, and when they introduced me to him, it was obvious that there was some tension. One of the managers gave the tech lead a back slap and said, "don't be too hard on the guy". The tech lead took me to a Chinese restaurant where I had some of the best food I've ever eaten. After a morning of little to no breakfast and continuous interviews, I was starving. He interviewed me as I ate, which is something I can't stand. I like to eat, and it is not easy for me to focus on talking shop when I'm enjoying lunch! Most of his questions focused on TCP/IP networking, which wasn't really what I wanted to do. I began to realize through this interview that the job may not be what I had expected. I was not a network engineer and did not want to be one. He proceeded to berate me about the fact that I had an MBA. "I hate MBA's" he said. "MBA's think they know everything" and started ranting and raving about managers. It did not take much to figure out he was referring to his two colleagues. At this point I realized that something was dreadfully wrong. The technical interview part was not that bad, just not what I expected, and it was obvious that this guy was in serious conflict with my two champions.

Once back at the office, I was sat in a room by myself for a while, and I could hear the tech lead arguing profusely with the other two managers I had talked to. I knew right then that I was wasting my time. The job was lost. But it really was not my fault. The two managers wanted someone entirely different from the tech lead. They were at war with him, and today was a decisive battle. Unfortunately, I was caught in the middle, and paying the price with my time.

I then met briefly with the manager who I had first talked to. He was all red-faced, and not happy at all. He was setting me up to interview with another tech lead who was supposed to be more amiable. At this point, I had decided that I did not want to work there. I had shut down my job interview engines, and was in standby mode waiting to be released. One mistake I made was that I did not realize that they were still trying to find a fit for me. As I interviewed with the second technical lead, he took his shoes off and I could smell his dirty socks. It was difficult to carry on a conversation because he kept typing. He, like all the other interviewers, was constantly sending instant messages to the others to figure out what to ask me next. This is something I've only seen at company x and I hate it. It's a bad practice and very distracting. I asked this guy questions about his job and it became obvious that this wasn't for me. He was doing nothing more than third-level technical support. I saw this as a low-level job. However, at company x, this was not so. Companies with highly proprietary technology often place a higher importance on lower level roles, because of their specialized nature. In any case, I didn't want it. At this point I then interviewed with the operations director, and in not so many words told him I wasn't interested. They seemed desperate to find a fit for me somewhere, but I did not hear anything after this. I did talk briefly with the human resources person, but her English was so bad I could not understand what she said.

Months later I interviewed again with company x, for an entirely different position. The process was much the same, except that the hiring manager seemed quite downtrodden and unhappy both over the phone and in person. Apparently, he was in the process of being demoted. He stated that I could probably just do a quick study of .NET on the plane to get past the interview! The tech lead interviewed me on the phone in the beginning and gave me the thumbs up, but when I arrived onsite to talk with him, we had a serious language barrier. We had two very different ways of breaking down and solving problems. I don't think either one of us was wrong, but we had too much difficulty communicating, and the methods were very different. These conditions deep-sixed the interview.

I put this experience in the "heaven" chapter because overall it was positive. They did not think twice about paying for my travel to send me out onsite, and once there, they wanted to make it work. Dysfunction between stakeholders got in the way, and it turned out to not be the kind of job I wanted anyhow.

INTERVIEW LESSON #12: Company x, like many companies similar in size and scope, often has unique job roles, interview processes, and expectations. It's almost like interviewing in a different country. Jobs at these companies can be good long-term careers, but the proprietary nature of the work, and specialized roles, can make it difficult to find employment elsewhere when the time comes. As mentioned previously, they often assign a higher value to lower level work, giving you an inflated sense of your marketability over time. If you take a job like this, you need to think seriously about how it will fit into your long-term plans.

The Investigator

I had an interview with a very large bank. They wanted a vice president for quality in their IT department. I interviewed with three people. The first, was the recruiter and human resources person who seemed a bit nervous. He talked very fast. I liked the job description and the company environment. I had discussed the salary with the recruiter in the beginning, and we settled on a pretty firm range. The second interview was with another VP who was also a technical interviewer. This interview went very well, and he added that he had researched me on LinkedIn and spoken with a mutual contact of ours to get a reference on me. The reference was fortunately positive. I realized that what others thought about me was considered important here. I then interviewed with the hiring manger, which was extensive. She asked me a lot of detailed questions, and it felt a bit like an interrogation. I learned that she was a lawyer by profession. She asked me the same question over and over but rephrased it differently each time. Despite this, I felt like the interview went smoothly. Afterwards, I overheard her tell the hiring manager that she wanted to hire me, and that I was the best candidate that they had talked to. She was so enthusiastic she didn't seem to care that I was within earshot. I thought "great!". Unfortunately, when it came time to make an offer, it was lower than even what I had discussed with the recruiter. He had no real explanation for this, and was a bit heavy-handed about it. I ended up taking another job that I had interviewed for at around the same time. As I have mentioned many times before, the best person does not always get the job, even the person that the hiring manager wants. For some reason, human resources stopped this, likely because my salary requirements put me at a higher level than one or more of the other employees. Why didn't they do this in the beginning? After all, we discussed salary. Because they wanted to burn my time to provide them with intelligence on where they stood in the market, and probably to impress the hiring manager.

INTERVIEW LESSON #13: Be sure your LinkedIn profile is up to date, and that you have good relations with your connections. Try to find out who your interviewers are beforehand and research them as well. The intel you gather could be invaluable.

Overall, I would say that "heaven" interviews are those which go smoothly. In just about every job interview that resulted in a good offer, there was never conflict, or stress, or challenge involved. If you are interviewed for a job which you are well-qualified for, and the company is genuinely looking to hire, and if you follow these suggestions, you will have a "job interview from heaven" that will result in a good offer. Don't waste time worrying about interviews that you know in your gut didn't go well. Don't stand by the mailbox waiting for that job. Learn from it, and move on.

CHAPTER FIVE

QUICK START GUIDE

I've developed this chapter as a stand-alone guide of sorts, for those who want to get down to the basics. If you don't read anything else, please read this guide.

GETTING THE INTERVIEW

The interview process for high-tech jobs is really an exercise in marketing oneself. You are marketing your skillset, your personality, your strengths, and even your weaknesses. You are marketing You! A successful interview takes more than just showing up on interview day with your résumé in hand. You will have to do some soul-searching, preparation and follow-up work to be truly successful.

Step 1: Know Yourself and the Market

The process of interviewing is truly an exercise in introspection. Just as a salesman is more effective in selling a product he knows, you must know your needs, wants, strengths and weaknesses to successfully market yourself to potential employers.

Honestly examine your skillset and the job requirements. Often, the descriptions posted on job boards are too vague, general, or too all-encompassing for one person to fulfill all the requirements. However, if you have a decent cross-section of the skills listed and a plan of action for acquiring any missing skills, you can create what amounts to a proposal for the employer: "Here's what I have, here's what I don't have, but I can get it by following this plan."

Look at the job market. What positions are available, what kind of salary does your chosen profession make in your area? If you can't find what you're looking for locally, are you willing to relocate? Take a holistic view of the jobs that interest you. What is the company culture like? What is the average work day like? What about travel and overtime? Examine the company benefits packages if you have that information available. Salary is just one part of the equation.

Be realistic about your strengths and limitations. If the job is looking for a senior engineer with 15 years of experience and a Ph.D. in particle physics, but you have just graduated from Awesome Tech. U, with a B.S. and experience with an internship in software development, that job is probably not the right fit for you. It is ok to reach a little, but again, be realistic with your goals and what you can accomplish. Every new job has a learning curve, but don't set yourself up for failure.

Step 2: Write Your Own Résumé

The process of writing your own résumé builds on Step 1. Résumé services offer to write your résumé, start to finish, with just a list of things you've done and skills you have. Using a service is fine, but nobody knows you as well as you do. It's more effective for you to get help with a product you had a hand in making than to have a résumé you barely touched. When you interview, rest assured that the prospective employer is going to ask you what you did, and if your answers don't mesh with the résumé, they will probably be able to tell.

Start building a master résumé. In this document, put down everything you've done, ever. Try to document the timeframe, who you worked for, and most importantly, any impact you had with the effort. Capture volunteer work, additional duties for employment, school projects, hobbies, tutoring, and anything else that could ever be construed as experience or skills.

Craft compelling narratives for projects, accomplishments, or achievements. Carefully select phrases using active voice and build a strong vocabulary of active verbs to convey your meaning.

For a recruiter to take your application seriously (or for the résumé to even make it past the automated screening process), your résumé absolutely must be tailored to the job you are applying for. Once you have the master résumé, read over the job ad, or position description and highlight requirements that you meet. Use keywords from the job description in filling out your accomplishments to the maximum extent possible, but in all cases, be honest.

Step 3: The HR Screening Interview

You did your soul-searching, you researched your market and targeted a job that fit your needs, goals, desires, and skillset. You crafted a résumé that is professional, polished and highlights your talents and experience. The recruiter at your targeted company likes what she sees in your résumé.

Now the recruiter is calling and asking questions about your résumé and your experience. This conversation is just one part of the multi-step technical interview process. You need to be prepared to describe your experiences in detail and demonstrate how your experience relates to the requirements in the job description. This is why you should write your own résumé and be very familiar with its contents. Reference back to your compelling narratives from the résumé-writing process and expand upon what you did. Often, the résumé format forces you to condense experience down to just a few short sentences, but the screening interview is your chance to really expand upon what you did and emphasize the impacts of your accomplishments.

Before Interview Day

Congratulations, your hard work has paid off! The recruiter called back and wants you to schedule an interview. Now what? This is where marketing yourself really comes in. If you think about it, your résumé is your product description, but your interview is the sales floor product demonstration. You've got to move on to Phase 2, The Interview.

Step 4: Know the Audience

If, by our analogy, the interview is your sales pitch, it makes sense that you should know your audience. In this case, the interviewer is your audience. Find out from the recruiter who your interviewer will be and find out the format. Is the interview a one-on-one interview or will you be in front of several people? Is the interview over the phone, via Skype or in person? What position or positions do your interviewers hold in the company? If possible, find out what kind of questions will be asked of you. Ask the recruiter directly and do some research online. There are more than a few websites that cater to job seekers by allowing users to post interview reviews and questions. Look at what others in your field have been asked. If possible, look up the company you work for and see what kind of questions they are asking. You may not run into the exact questions, but at least you will have a clue with regards to the type, technical depth, and number of questions.

Do some research on your interviewers and the company you interview with. Look up the interviewers on LinkedIn, Google+, Facebook, Twitter, GitHub, Stack Exchange, or other professional and social networking platforms. You can learn a lot about the interviewer's background, experience, and interests. Use this information, if available, to help with creating your compelling narratives of experience and skills. If you know your audience, you can be more effective in presenting yourself in a meaningful way to them.

Write down a few questions about the company and the job in a notebook that you can bring with you to the interview. Be sure to think about the kind of problems this company is solving in creating your questions. Well-thought-out questions can show the interviewer that you are prepared. Questions about company culture are also good questions.

Step 5: Know your skills

Since you are interviewing for a position in technology, be sure to brush up on the basics of your field. For example, a software engineer will most likely have to answer some basic questions about the language they work in and may also be asked to implement a solution to a small problem on a white board. Network engineers and IT professionals may be asked to create a solution to an enterprise engineering task and explain their rationale.

Look at your field of expertise and think about how you would be able to tell if someone knows the field beyond the job description. Work through and rehearse the problem-solving process using sound reasoning and techniques. Brush up on the basics of your field, if necessary, consider some online courses to help with the refresh. Get up to speed on the state of the art. Know what the trends in your field are and look for ways to keep current.

Step 6: *Practice, Practice, Practice*

If describing your experiences during the HR screening was challenging for you, this is your chance to really polish up. Preparation for an interview requires a few things. First, prepare an "Elevator Speech". What would you say to someone in an elevator if they said, "Tell me about yourself?" This is not the time to talk about your pets or your most embarrassing childhood experience. It IS an opportunity to make a good impression with that person regarding your experience, goals, and skills. It's important for you to have your elevator speech well-rehearsed, polished, and high-impact. The interviewer will almost certainly ask you to tell them about yourself sometime during the process, be prepared.

Review your résumé and polish up the compelling narratives that describe your experiences and skills. As a general rule, you should be able to explain everything on your résumé without much hesitation. Remember, this is the time to highlight your accomplishments. Make sure to keep your descriptions in the first person. One pitfall to avoid is "we-talk". If you catch yourself saying "My team built this component. We designed that widget and we solved such-and-such problem," you need to work hard on focusing your narrative on your contribution. It is ok to refer to the overall situation as a team, but the interviewer is really interested in how YOU can benefit their company, not how your team benefitted your previous company. It cannot be stressed enough; your presentation of your skills is the primary purpose of the interview. This step is called Practice, Practice, Practice because practice is the key to success. You are only hurting yourself if the interview is the first time you ever describe what you have done to another person.

Practice your narratives in front of a mirror. Take note of your facial expressions, mannerisms, and nervous movements. Ask a friend or colleague to give you a mock interview and to critique your responses both verbal and nonverbal.

Lastly, write down some non-technical questions you think might be asked. A very common question goes something like this, "Tell me about a time when you failed at a project." Use this as a chance to show how you work through problems, how you contribute to a team, and how you as a person and a professional can grow in the face of adversity. Other common questions revolve around how you function in a team and what you do in various situations.

Step 7: The Interview

All of the work you have done should prepare you for this moment. Remember to bring copies of your résumé and your notebook with questions about the company and the job. Relax, you've done a good job. You're going to do fine. Arrive a few minutes early, so you're not rushed or stressed. Rehearse your elevator speech while you wait and go over your compelling narratives from your résumé. If the interviewer is amenable to the idea, take notes during the interview.

When you are asked a question, take your time, think through your responses, and then begin responding. Again, if permissible, take a note about the question, mainly to compose yourself. If you don't know an answer, especially to a technical question, be up-front and say so. Talk through the process of solving the problem. You may reach the correct solution, or you may not, however, an interviewer will often be evaluating the way you solve problems as much as whether you know the answer to problems. Even if you know the answer immediately, it may be beneficial to work through the problem.

After the Interview

Even though the interview is complete, you still have some work to do. The post-interview phase is critical to your growth. Even if you don't get a call back from this company, you still can leverage everything you've learned and experienced in this process.

Step 8: Capture the Details

Immediately after the interview, take a few moments to take notes on your perception of the interview. Make sure you know the name of the interviewer. Regardless of your performance, write down what was asked of you and what you answered. Remember, every interview, good or bad, is a chance to learn and grow. If you did not know an answer to a question, be sure to find it out. Certainly, take notes on what you think you could do better next time as there is always room for improvement.

Step 9: Follow Up

Consider sending a note written on real paper, thanking the interviewer or team for their time. It's a simple thing, but it can make an impression regarding your thoughtfulness and follow-through. This is a judgement call, but if the interviewer seemed amenable to communication after the interview, consider answering the questions you didn't know and sending those answers in a well-thought-out manner to the interviewer. It may or may not affect their decision process, but it will show dedication and it will help YOU learn and grow. Review your notes and make sure you know the answers to questions that may have tripped you up. When you get a call back from the company, it can only help you to know the answer to those questions.

Step 10: Improve and Iterate

As a professional in a technical field, you have probably learned about process improvement techniques. Apply those principles to your interview skills. It is a rare person who is successful in every interview. If you "Aced" it, there is still room for improvement. Even if you didn't get the job, by being prepared, taking notes and practicing, you've just made preparation for your next interview that much easier. Like most things in life, the improvement process is an iterative process. Take what you learned about yourself, about the job type, about the interviewers' mindsets and apply that toward crafting the best interview strategy you can. With practice, you can be familiar enough yourself and the process to do on-the-spot interviews at job fairs, or anywhere you happen to have the opportunity.

When the process is over, all that is left for you to do is to wait for word back from the company. If you did well, there may be follow-up interviews or additional interviews: Many companies use multi-step interviews. This is where the self-improvement part of the interview process is extremely important. You may be asked clarifying questions, or if you were successful and got a job offer, your skills at interviewing and expressing your value to the company can be used for negotiating salary and benefits. The interview process is about marketing yourself, make the most of every opportunity you get in the process to make yourself even more marketable.

CHAPTER SIX

AFTER THE OFFER

Salary Negotiation

Salary negotiation is arguably the most important business technique to getting a professional job. After all, we don't work for free! Your salary is more than just money, it determines your visibility within an organization, and is a monetary statement of your value to the company. Higher-paid people typically get the most important projects, have the most visibility with upper management, and are the first in line for job grade promotions.

Despite all of this, many people, even seasoned professionals in their field, fail to obtain good salary negotiation techniques. Often, the highest paid person in the group isn't necessarily the smartest or the best at their jobs, they are just the best at convincing management and HR that they are! Much of this technique comes with changing jobs often. After all, if you've worked for the same company for twenty years, you are extremely experienced in your field and probably have high rank in your organization, but chances are you don't know squat about salary negotiation because you've never had to do it!! So, if such a person were to interview with another company, they will almost never get the money they want. On the other hand, someone with only about 5-10 years' experience could easily make more money than a person with twice the knowledge and experience, simply because they've changed jobs every two years, thus gaining knowledge and experience in salary negotiation as well as outside the "bubble" in which the ubiquitous "lifer" is confined.

Are you the highest-paid person in your group? If you aren't, then you need to keep reading, because you don't know as much as you think…. obviously!

Determining your worth

Before you sell a car or a house what is the first thing you do? Determine how much it's worth and create a selling price. Often, your asking price is higher than what you would actually accept. Selling yourself is very similar. You must determine your asking price, and your "walk away" price. To develop your asking price, I recommend using the following formula:

Current Compensation (CC) = (Current base salary + current annual bonus)

Asking Price (AP) = CC + .1(CC)

When determining your current compensation, always include your annual bonus or any other bonuses you get during the year! Never accept a base salary that is less than your TOTAL previous compensation! If your prospective employer asks you what your salary was, give them the TOTAL! Never give them your base pay… you'll get screwed for sure! Always ask for at least 10% over this total. If you don't get something close to that, it's not worth the trouble for you to change jobs. If you are unemployed, then that's another issue altogether. You may want to set your sights lower. The problem with that is, once you are on the job for a while and get comfortable, you may find that you are making much less than your counterparts, who may not be as good as you are. As a result, you'll end up in another job search. There are other job aspects to consider as well, such as commute, environment, responsibility, etc. But if you don't get at least a 10% raise in base pay, then you will eventually regret leaving your old job. By this method, you can almost always be sure that your BASE salary will be 10% more!

- Try to find out the pay range for the job. Make sure your asking price is in range.
- Never tell them your true current base salary! If they ask you for it, give them the salary plus any yearly bonuses you receive. Remember, employers can verify your employment, but salary is confidential…if you lie about your salary, it is not easy for them to find out without your permission.
- If you have a strong salary history and fear that you are in for a cut, use your salary history to your advantage! Show how many jobs and for how long you are making a certain amount of money. Build a "case" for your asking price!
- Do not disclose the fact that you are unemployed. You will get lowballed…if you are out of work and don't want to lie, tell them that you are currently working for yourself…. for god sakes, don't tell them that you are broke and out of a job. You will get screwed. I did work for an organization once that actively sought out people who were "down and out" and believed that these candidates worked harder. However, this is rare.
- Play it cool and firm. Know what you want and stick to your guns. Any waffling or indecision will be interpreted as a sign of weakness on your part and they will offer less.
- Get multiple offers, and play them against each other.

Answering the "questions"

Most companies will ask you questions to gain information to weaken your position. Some examples are listed below. You may recognize many of these questions from your own interview experiences.

1. What's the lowest you will take? Give them a figure between your walk away and asking prices.

2. I have an offer for X amount of money, it's not what you asked for, but I can try to get more if you want. If I try to get you more money and fail, will you turn this job down? Say "yes". The HR rep is trying to determine your resolve. Let them "think" that you won't take less…if they fail in getting more, you can always accept their previous offer.

3. Are you currently interviewing with other companies? "Yes, but I just started looking. Your company is my first interview!" If they think you've been to several interviews but haven't had an offer, they will feel insecure about making you an offer themselves. If they think you are "fresh meat" and a good catch that no one has had a chance to hook, they will be more likely to make an offer.

4. How many offers have you received? This is private information and very "forward". Try not to become indignant. Politely decline to answer directly. If you have received offers, say "yes" I am considering other offers, but I am mostly interested in your company for XXX reasons. Or, if you haven't had any offers, simply say that you are not really conducting a full-scale job search, you are simply interested in the particular opportunity that the company is offering at this time.

5. If you had offers from multiple companies, which one would you accept? Yours, of course! Always let the company think that THEIR company is the place you want to work! If you indicate that you prefer another company, then they won't even try to make an offer.

6. Will you accept the job now? Tell them you'd like to sleep on it or talk it over with your family. Don't cave to high-pressure sales! Always give yourself 24hrs to consider any job change.

CHAPTER SEVEN

INTERVIEW DO'S AND DON'TS

There are the usual do's and don'ts for job interviews that many of us know about, that you can find on the internet. Take a shower, dress well, have good eye contact, etc. In keeping with the Big Brother's objective of providing "uncommon knowledge", the following do's and don'ts are those which you probably have not been exposed to, but are even more important in today's world.

Do

1. Smile, be friendly. But don't overdo it. You want to give the impression that you want the job, but you will be ok without it.

2. Pay close attention to the questions you are being asked and give concise answers. An old interview trick is to ask a person the same question twice to see if they give a different answer. If they do this to you, call them out on it and then repeat your previous answer.

3. Follow up on the interview, especially if you think it went well. Don't say too much though. Just offer thanks for the opportunity and willingness to answer any further questions they have. Drop in a line or two extolling some of the positive

points during the interview.

4. Assess each person you talk to. You will have to work with these people, and a bad feeling about someone will most likely turn into a problem later.

5. Ask about the roles and responsibilities in detail and make sure you understand them. Often, the job descriptions mean nothing.

6. Try to get a tour of the facility, especially of where your peers would be located. Get a sense of the work environment, and observe closely what everyone is doing. Ask yourself, "does this look like a place you want to work?"

7. Try as best as you can to figure out if they are seriously trying to fill the job. Very often, your time will be wasted because a key decision-maker has already decided to give the job to an internal applicant, the role is on the verge of being canceled, or no one can agree on who to hire. Inevitably, in any job search, much of your time is going to be wasted, but if you pay close attention to the cues, you may be able to reduce this. The less time you waste on dead ends, the more time you have to focus on real opportunities.

8. Ask for the job but don't expect it. Most companies are required to interview other candidates, and perform a number of checks before making an offer.

9. Apply to as many jobs as you can. Getting a job is a game of numbers, the more darts you throw, the better chances something will stick.

10. Focus on quality opportunities that make sense with your career goals and your résumé. Frivolous applications will be a waste of time.

Don't

1. Come on too strong. I interviewed a woman one time that shook and squeezed my hand so hard I thought she would

break it. She was trying to show enthusiasm, but it translated into desperation and awkwardness.

2. Argue with the interviewer, or appear combative. One time when I asked a question during an interview, the candidate replied, "the answer is on my résumé". I knew that, but I wanted to see what she'd say to the question. I was testing her. Sometimes people's résumés aren't true.

3. Give them your true salary. Give them a range instead. They will almost always give you an offer that is at or near the bottom of your range, or is less than what you are currently making. With most companies these days, the objective is to get the cheapest person that can fill the job, not the best. They don't want Cadillac's, only Chevy's.

4. Don't be too hard on yourself if you don't get the job. All too often, there are internal problems and dysfunctions that make your success impossible. I interviewed a candidate with a co-worker of mine who I knew was prejudiced with lots of strange ideas. She told the boss the candidate had "crazy eyes" whenever she asked him a question. The real reason was her questions were stupid and he was taken off guard. However, the boss believed my colleague and the candidate lost out.

5. Don't go to an interview sick. No matter how bad you want the job, no one is going to give you kudos for showing up, or cut you slack on the technical interview because you had a headache. If you don't feel good, reschedule it. They will assume that what they are seeing is the best of you, even if it isn't.

6. Don't be late. No matter what. Excuses don't help here. If you have even the smallest inkling that the traffic or weather will hold you up, leave extra early or reschedule. Yeah, you might have to sit in a nearby coffee shop for a long time if you make it too early, but if you are already spending your personal time on the interview, why not do it right?

7. Don't boast, either about personal aspects or your professional achievements. Mention them if you must, but do so humbly. People are more insecure than ever today.

8. Don't curse, even if the interviewer does it. People tend to notice the indiscretions of others, while conveniently turning a blind eye to their own. "Mirroring" your interviewer can be a good technique, but do so with the positive traits, not everything.

9. Say anything negative about a current or previous boss or company.

10. Say anything negative about yourself, even in a light-hearted, self-deprecating sort of way. Anything you say can and will be used against you.

CHAPTER EIGHT

SUMMARY

Interviewing is often more about presentation than substance. After all, how much can you really learn about a person in only an hour? It should also be noted that interviews for jobs in the computer business, or "techie" interviews, are different from most. Technical positions often have requirements that are difficult to define, and Managers of such groups may be looking for special "qualities" as opposed to brute skill.

Look the part

Make no mistake, dressing well is essential. I don't care what anyone tells you. Yes, it is true that today's business environment is much more relaxed, and the lack of a suit is not as unacceptable as it once was. However, it is always much safer to come dressed professionally, otherwise, you will risk offending somebody. Show respect, dress accordingly.

Be prepared for the obvious questions

Always have a prepared speech ready for any of the questions below:

1. Tell us about yourself.

2. Where do you see yourself in five years?

3. Why did you leave your last job?

4. Why do you want to work here?

5. Tell us about a recent success.

6. Tell us about a recent failure. Why did you fail? Try to turn failures into a positive, focusing on what you learned from it.

7. Be aware of any specific technical questions common to your profession.

Practice – Interview often

Practice makes perfect, and this is even more true with interviewing. Interview as much as you can. The more you interview, the better you will become at fielding questions. The knowledge you gain will enhance your comfort level and translate into more confidence. This will show come interview time.

Know the job requirements

Be sure that you are familiar with each requirement of the job, and that you have ready-made answers as to how your background meets each one. If the description lists "desired skills" or "pluses", be sure to harp on these as much as possible, if you have them.

Know your résumé

Many managers will interview you simply by using your résumé. Often, this gives them the best clue as to how knowledgeable you really are. Be sure that you can give examples of how you used each skill listed, and are ready to explain any accomplishment, or technology that your résumé contains.

Beating the technical interview – Avant-Garde techniques

Attempting to beat the interview can be a successful strategy, but only if you are skilled. Be advised that using these types of techniques may cost you the job as quickly as you could win it, depending on your interviewers' demeanor. Using these techniques effectively takes great practice and skill, but they do work. The reason they work is because with technical interviews, there's almost always something they could ask you that you don't know, no matter how good you are. Plus, if you interview with several people, as most end up doing, chances are one of them is going to be an asshole. You want to bury this guy/gal and prevent them from eliminating you. These are techniques for doing so. If you sense this coming your way, these methods can get you past the "blocker".

Talking them to death

This technique involves overloading the interviewer with information. Each time they ask you a question, you make your answer as long and as involved as possible. Interviewers usually only have so much time. By "filibustering", you limit the number of questions the interviewer can ask, hence making it less likely that he will ask you a hard question you can't answer. In addition, it also makes him so tired that he is ready to quit. Observe politicians when they are being interviewed on TV. Often, they don't answer the question directly and take the answer into and entirely different vein.

Interview Hijacking

This is where you start asking the questions. This puts the interviewer on the defensive. In addition, if you keep it up, the interviewer won't have time to get through his entire question list. Again, this is a good technique if you are afraid that the interviewer will ask a technical question you can't answer. Care must be taken here to not appear too aggressive. You want to win the interviewer over. Take control, but be polite about it. Disguise your efforts as being enthusiastic about the job. Redirect the conversation to topics with which you are familiar.

Buddy, buddy

If you are charismatic enough, perhaps you can win over the interviewer by sheer force of personality. By working it right, you will spend your interview talking about your kids and the latest fishing trip you went on, instead of answering tough questions about java servlets. You've got to be good to pull this one off, and often it's one of those things that just happens because you have a good personality match with the interviewer. Being an attractive example of the opposite sex helps immensely. It does work.

Most job interviews consist of several interviewers, many of whom are not the key decision-makers and provide only marginal input. In such cases, the interviewer has the potential to eliminate people, but little input to select their favorite. As a result, these avant-garde techniques can be helpful – assisting you in getting past the "gauntlet" so you can focus on the final goal, the decision-maker.

Interview Situations to Avoid

If you feel that the interviewer is angry, rude, offensive, prejudiced or whatever, get up and leave. You don't have to put up with that abuse. Remember, if someone is acting that way, you won't get hired. Period. So, don't waste your time. Be sure to report them to the HR department before you leave, or shortly after. Be tactful and objective about it. You want to avoid making yourself look partly to blame.

Handling the Tech Lead

Interviewing with the technical lead is different from talking to the manager. The technical lead is there because, for one reason or another, the manager does not feel like he/she has the expertise to effectively "tech you out", or wants buy-in from others on the team. However, the technical lead's main goal, is to make sure that you won't take their job. So, what you need to do, is answer every technical question as well as possible, but concentrate on making a friend out of this person. You want to make him/her understand that you won't do anything to threaten their position. Be careful not to look "too good" in front of the Tech Lead...otherwise, you won't get hired. Express reliability, but vulnerability.

Before the interview is over, be sure to:

1. Fill out an application.
2. Get the business cards of everyone you talked to.
3. Get the hiring manager's email address
4. Ask for the job.
5. Find out when you can expect a response.

Probe for Issues

Remember that you are also interviewing the company! You need to make sure that the position is a good fit for you and that it will meet your career goals and objectives. More importantly though, probe for problems. You can't be too careful these days and need to make sure of what you are walking into. Be aware of managers that seem too eager to hire for the wrong reasons. Ask questions like these:

1. How long have you been working for company X?
2. What challenges have you been facing here at company X?
3. What are you looking for in a candidate?
4. How many people are on your team currently? How long have they been here?

The main danger signals you want to look out for is high turnover, financial instability, bad unstable bosses, and political strife. These things can kill an organization, at best, stunt your professional growth, and at worst, make you hate your job and profession.

I believe that if you put to use all the lessons learned in this volume, you will get more high-quality interviews, reduce time spent on your job search, and land more offers. I wish you the best in your quest for better employment. It's out there. Don't let anyone discourage you. Long ago one manager told me as he walked me out the door on my last day, "it's not going to be any better anywhere else". He could not have been more wrong. I have had many good jobs better than that one and each change I have made has been better than the last. That manager is now so senile he does not recognize me. Do not listen to people like that. Make your own way. Get good advice. Remember, your Big Brother is always here for you.

Photo: Stuart Hasson

ABOUT THE AUTHOR

Dr. David A. Bishop is a technologist, systems/solutions architect, consultant, researcher, entrepreneur, and instructor with over 25 years of experience in telecommunications, transportation, airline, government, and utility industries. David holds a Bachelor of Computer Engineering degree from the Georgia Institute of Technology, an MBA with a concentration in IT management, and a Doctorate in Business Administration from Georgia State University. He is an inventor of five U.S. patents.

Dr. Bishop is the creator of agile vortex theory, which is the subject of his forthcoming book, *"Metagility: Managing Agile Development for Competitive Advantage"* and a regular contributor to engineering and management publications worldwide. He is a member and committee chair for the International Electrotechnical Commission based in Geneva, Switzerland, a member of the ACM, and a Senior Member of the **IEEE**.

ABOUT OUR BIG BROTHER SERIES

Wish you had a big brother or sister to talk to for advice? REAL advice that you can use based on rich experience and solid research? The Big Brother Guides are a new series of books with a common theme and format designed to serve as self help tools for life and business issues. We don't sell "dummies" or "idiots" guides because we don't believe you are one. Big Brother Guides are for smart people like YOU! One of the biggest complaints about many similar books on the market today is that they are written by no name authors with no credentials and little to no experience. Big Brother Guides are written by knowledgeable and experienced authors who are bona fide experts in their field, not by some dude that just has a blog or YouTube channel. With the Big Brother's Guides, you get uncommon knowledge and even peer reviewed research. You can have confidence in Big Brother, and more importantly, get the kind of information that only a good mentor with your best interests at heart can provide. If you don't have a REAL big brother you can rely on for advice, we've got one for you!

Have confidence big bro has gotchyo back!

Big Brother Guides: Uncommon Knowledge for the Masses, validated through research and written by experts...for smart people like YOU!

Check us out at: www.bigbrotherguides.com

www.ingramcontent.com/pod-product-compliance
Lightning Source LLC
Chambersburg PA
CBHW031225090426
42740CB00007B/710